THE WIT
OF
MUSIC

Enrico Caruso
London
1906

THE WIT
OF
MUSIC

Compiled by Leslie Ayre

With an Introduction by
Sir John Barbirolli

LESLIE FREWIN : LONDON

1. Music - Anecdotes, facetiae, satire etc. I. Title

780.7
A 984 W

First published 1966
by Leslie Frewin Publishers Limited,
15 Hay's Mews, Berkeley Square, London, W.1.
Printed by Anchor Press,
and bound by Wm. Brendon,
both of Tiptree, Essex

Contents

62137

Introduction by
Sir John Barbirolli

I AM happy to have been asked to write an introduction to *The Wit of Music*, as I have for some time thought that such a book should be compiled. Indeed, I myself have one or two stories to offer.

While crossing the Atlantic, Toscanini and I met in the lounge, where I was studying Bartok's masterpiece, *Music for Strings, Percussion and Celeste*, of which I was to give the New York première. The score, with constant changes of tempo, looked something like this:

$$\tfrac{2}{8} \quad \tfrac{11}{4} \quad \tfrac{13}{8} \quad \tfrac{7}{8} \quad \tfrac{1}{4} \text{ etc.}$$

'Interesting,' said Toscanini. 'Looks like Tombola.'

My old friend Erich Kleiber, rehearsing *Rosenkavalier* on a cold morning at Covent Garden, was vainly trying to get some *schmaltz* from the violins. 'Ah well,' he said eventually, 'perhaps vibrato will come with dinner jacket.'

And I remember conducting *Aïda* in Leeds in the late 'twenties. It was rather a charming old theatre, though primitive in its backstage facilities – the ladies' toilet was just above the prompt side of the stage. In the last act, the entombed Radames sang the *unaccompanied* recitative,

Introduction

Aïda, where art thou now? – and immediately the ancient and sonorous plug was vigorously pulled. I'm afraid the opera ended there, though we continued gallantly to the end!

Overture

WHEN SOMEONE made so bold as to point out to Melba that she made more money in a year than the President of the United States, she replied in the properly grand manner of the diva. 'Then why,' she demanded, 'why doesn't he sing?'

But just a moment. Was it Melba — or was it Patti? That is what happens to stories about people who become legendary figures. Stories of the old days have a way of *attaching* themselves to people. It is still possible today — but much less probable.

What is certain is that a sense of fun is common to most of the great artists of today and of yesterday. This may depart far from the idea of the 'serious' musician being long-haired and desperately intense *all the time*. Living in the heights is all very fine — but the belly-laugh or the quiet chuckle have a place of great importance.

It may seem irreverent that members of the orchestra, after a stiff evening's playing in *Das Rheingold*, accompany the great closing tune with the words, 'Thank God, we're nearly through'. It fits splendidly and it is a mark of their professionalism that it should come into their minds.

When *Götterdämmerung* was being recorded recently, and Birgit Nilsson (Brünnhilde) called for her fiery steed,

---

Grane, a horse was led – much to her surprise – into the studio. It stopped the proceedings.

And not so long ago at Covent Garden, during rehearsal of *Fidelio*, there came the great moment when Rocco, the jailer, hands over the key for the devoted wife to free her husband. Gottlob Frick produced from his sleeve a massive key that was almost too heavy for the soprano to hold. Again there was a break for a laugh.

Is that sort of thing a waste of time? Of course not. Tensions and temperaments run high on these occasions. The laugh brings valuable relief.

Great composers of the past nearly all seized upon the moments of relief. It is pleasant, for instance, to think of Mozart writing to his wife that, during a performance of *The Magic Flute*, he had slipped into the wings and played the offstage glockenspeil in the wrong places, much to the discomforture of the Papageno on the stage.

Or of Rossini, sitting among a group of friends, when his manservant announced that a well-known tenor was asking to see him. 'Certainly,' said Rossini. 'But please ask him to leave his top note outside with his hat and stick. He may of course collect it again as he leaves.'

Or of the same Rossini saying, 'Give me a laundry list and I'll set it to music.'

In our own time, Beecham was the master wag. He has a section to himself in this book but his goatee beard insists upon jutting in all the time. There is nothing else for it. When musicians get talking about the lighter things, Beecham just has to be there.

One ought, of course, to be able to hear the suave, courteous voice and to see the occasional knowing wink. He could say things to his orchestra which no other conductor would dare utter. Far from falling out, they adored him – because they knew that he had a great love for orchestral players.

Two of his most effective approaches were those of exaggeration and of surprise. When he was rehearsing for his last appearance at Covent Garden, I asked him, expecting the obvious answer, whether he was all prepared to deal with any latecomers or chatterers. 'Not at all,' he said. 'Delighted to see them if they care to drop in at their convenience – providing of course that they change into carpet-slippers in the foyer.'

And when he turned up to open an exhibition of books on music in London, he started by announcing: 'There are *no* good books on music.'

But the point was made – that one does not learn about music simply by reading books about it. Isaac Stern has made the same point in different words: 'Learning music by reading about it is like making love by mail.'

They are engaging people, the musicians – and, usually, the bigger they are the more sense of fun they have – generally of the dry order.

LESLIE AYRE

Conductors

ORCHESTRAL CONDUCTORS in the main are a long-lived fraternity. Toscanini and Monteux, for instance, were eighty-nine and Beecham eighty-two. Among those still active in the concert hall, Stokowski is at the time of writing eighty-four, Ansermet eighty-two, Klemperer eighty-one, Boult seventy-seven, Sargent seventy-one and Barbirolli a mere sixty-six. It seems that the secret is that they must be initially blessed with unusual stamina and vitality and that, once they *are* conductors, the daily exercise keeps them fit:

'If you want a cure for a cold, put on two pullovers, take up a baton, poker or pencil, tune the radio to a symphony concert, stand on a chair, and conduct like mad for an hour or so and the cold will have vanished. It never fails. You know why conductors live so long? Because we perspire so much.'

Sir John Barbirolli

*　　　*　　　*

'I smoked my first cigarette and kissed my first woman at a very early age. Since then I have never smoked.'

Arturo Toscanini

*　　　*　　　*

'I have an energetic job. I spend up to six hours a day waving my arms about and if everyone else did the same they would stay much healthier. I don't have to play golf to get exercise. When I'm not working I put up my feet and relax.'

Sir Malcolm Sargent

*   *   *

'I gave a heavyweight boxer a baton weighing only half an ounce. "Wave that about and see how long you can keep it up," I told him. He did it for nine minutes and could not go on any longer.'

Sir Thomas Beecham

*   *   *

One phrase of Sir Henry Wood's became very familiar to the orchestra – 'What are you a-doin' of!' to express dissatisfaction at the way things were going.

On one occasion he snapped out merely 'What are you a-doin'!' There was a pause and then, as with one voice, the entire orchestra sang out the single word 'OF!'

Wood chuckled.

*   *   *

Sidney Harrison, in his book *The Artless Musician*, holds out a cheering prospect for those embarking on a conducting career: 'With any luck you will marry your fourth young woman when you are seventy and will fall off the rostrum at ninety-two.'

But clearly there are occupational hazards to the job. When nearly eighty, Beecham was rehearsing for a concert at Carnegie Hall, New York, when he noticed that the rail at the back of the rostrum was wobbly. He addressed the Philadelphia Orchestra: 'Whoever is trying to get rid of me had better accept the fact that I propose to go on conducting for at least another seventy years.'

*　　*　　*

Sir Henry Wood was an amazing and tireless man – working at scores, conducting, rehearsing, teaching singing, painting in water-colours, chopping down trees, making his own furniture.

Shortly before the war, Arturo Toscanini gave a performance of Beethoven's *Ninth 'Choral' Symphony* in London and soon afterwards Wood was giving the same work, with the same orchestra and soloists. He insisted that he must have five rehearsals but it was pointed out to him that, because of various circumstances, it was not possible to have more than three. But Wood was adamant.

'But,' it was stressed, 'Toscanini had only three rehearsals not so long ago with the same artists.'

'Really,' replied Wood. 'Perhaps *he* gets tired.'

*   *   *

When in his eighties, Pierre Monteux signed a twenty-five years' contract as principal conductor of the London Symphony Orchestra – on the strict condition that he could have an option for another twenty-five years!

*   *   *

After Beecham had given a performance of a Mozart opera in New York, conductor Fritz Reiner, who had been in the audience, went round to congratulate him.

'Thank you for a delightful evening with Beecham and Mozart,' said Reiner.

'Why drag in Mozart?' murmured Sir Thomas.

*   *   *

'On matters of intonation and technicalities I am more than a martinet – I am a martinetissimo.'

Leopold Stokowski

*   *   *

'Masterpieces are masterpieces because they are worth looking at from various points of view. There is always something new to discover about them. It is possible for several different performances to be given of a master-piece – all of them more or less 'right'. But there are even more ways of getting it wrong!'

Eduard van Beinum

*   *   *

Though Wilhelm Fürtwängler had an extraordinarily magnetic power over an orchestra, the outside observer often wondered how on earth the players managed to follow his beat. Indeed, it was not so much a beat as a convulsive trembling.

When he was making his debut at La Scala, Milan, he as usual started to shake all over as he was about to start the overture.

The leader of the orchestra leaned forward. 'Coraggio, signore!' he whispered.

*   *   *

Sir Landon Ronald, conductor, composer and for many years principal of the Guildhall School of Music in London, was out on tour with an orchestra, giving concerts with the same programme in several different towns and opening with Mendelssohn's *Midsummer Night's Dream* overture.

At one centre it was pointed out to him that another orchestra had played the Mendelssohn work only a few evenings earlier. He agreed to substitute the *Tannhäuser* overture.

Unfortunately, on the evening of the concert, he forgot about the change, with the result that, when he started the piece, he was greeted not by the delicate wood wind chords of Mendelssohn but by the very different voice of Wagner. He fainted on the rostrum.

Sir Landon said afterwards: 'It was like treading on a stair that wasn't there!'

Sir Landon loved telling stories against himself, many of them concerned with his generously proportioned nose.

On one occasion, so he said, he was peering into the small window of a concert-hall box-office to make an enquiry, when the assistant snapped out, 'If you'll take your elbow out of the way I might be able to tell what you want!'

*   *   *

Sir Malcolm Sargent has of course known for years that his nickname is 'Flash Harry'. In every season of Promenade Concerts at the Royal Albert Hall he is reminded of it by the 'Prommers' who call out 'We want Flash!'

It all started, Sir Malcolm has recalled, when he had been appearing on the BBC *Brains Trust* and immediately afterwards the announcer said that they were going over to a concert conducted by him – like a flash.

Some time afterwards, when Beecham heard that Sir Malcolm had been conducting highly successful concerts in Tokyo, he remarked: 'Flash in Japan, eh!'

On another occasion, Sir Malcolm had been recalling, in a speech at a dinner, that while conducting during the troubled times in Israel he had been fired on by Arabs. 'I had not realised that the Arabs were so musical,' murmured Sir Thomas.

(As a matter of fact, Sir Malcolm and Sir Thomas were close friends through the years. They shared the same birthday – though not of the same year – and never failed to exchange greetings.)

*   *   *

'I was born Giovanni Battista Barbirolli. My father was Italian but I was born within the sound of Bow Bells, so I've always looked on myself as a Cockney.

'It was during the 1914–18 war that I decided to change my name. I was an acting, unpaid lance-corporal in charge of gas masks. Each morning the sergeant major had great difficulty in reading my name on the roll-call.

' "Who is this Guy Vanni?" he used to ask. So I chose John.'

Sir John Barbirolli

*   *   *

During a rehearsal, Koussevitsky had a violent disagreement with one of the members of the orchestra and ordered him off the platform.

As the man walked away, he turned and called out: 'Nuts to you!'

'No, no,' insisted Koussevitsky. 'It's too late to apologise!'

*   *   *

One of the members of the Hallé Orchestra was fined for parking his car outside Huddersfield Town Hall in his anxiety not to be late for the rehearsal. He said to the magistrate:

'I prefer to face the wrath of the police rather than the wrath of Sir John Barbirolli.'

*   *   *

Shortly before a visit to London, Leopold Stokowski, then in his very late seventies, had been watching some youngsters playing football and had taken a flying kick at the ball, damaging his ankle.

He was leaning heavily on a stick when he arrived and caused some surprise by announcing that he had decided to retire.

'Yes,' he said, 'I have decided at last to retire – from football.'

His old friend Sir Eugene Goossens was conducting at the Royal Albert Hall and, at the interval, Stokowski looked in to see him. They immediately got themselves involved in a heated discussion about the best seating of the different sections of the orchestra.

'You see,' said Stokowski, 'Gene and I disagree about everything – except one thing – that all the women in Brazil are beautiful!'

*   *   *

'I am often asked who is my favourite composer. And I am sometimes even asked, "What is the most beautiful piece of music in the world?" To the latter I reply with another question: "Who is the most beautiful woman in the world?"'

Eduard van Beinum

*   *   *

Viennese-born Josef Krips – with his round face and glinting spectacles he looks like a taller version of Mr Pickwick – enjoys smoking very large cigars.

'I have ten of these a day – the first of them at 7 am,' he says. 'And there's one thing about it – if ever I lose my baton there'll always be one of these handy!'

José Iturbi, conductor as well as pianist, *has* been known to use a cigar-stub as baton at a rehearsal.

*   *   *

On arrival at a hotel in the United States, Pierre Monteux was told that it was for coloured people only.

'But I *am* coloured,' insisted Monteux. 'Pink!'

On another occasion, there had been a mix-up in hotel bookings and Monteux found himself without a room. Eventually the manager realised his identity and, pointing out that he had not known that he was 'somebody', said that arrangements could be made.

'Everybody is somebody,' said Monteux – and walked out.

*   *   *

In a town on Britain's south coast Beecham was appearing as guest conductor with an orchestra not his own. The orchestral manager impressed upon them the distinction of their guest and reminded them that white ties would be worn for the concert in the evening.

At the end of the rehearsal, Beecham thanked the orchestra – and added, with a grin, 'And don't forget, gentlemen – whitish ties!'

* * *

When offered a large floral wreath after a performance, Toscanini waved it aside.

'They are for *prima donnas* or corpses,' he said. 'I am neither.'

* * *

Despite his rather forbidding demeanour, Otto Klemperer is far from lacking a sense of humour. If at a rehearsal the brass, for instance, are not needed in the next work, Klemperer may well take out his handkerchief and wave them a mock farewell.

At a recording session of the Philharmonia Orchestra, the violas, not being required for a particular section, retired to another part of the studio.

In due course Klemperer called out: 'Violas, please!' They did not hear him. Then, imperiously, 'Come back, violas!' No response.

At last he pleaded, 'Come back, violas. All is forgiven.'

'I am the last of my classical school – when Bruno Walter died I put up my fee.'

Otto Klemperer

*　　*　　*

Rudolf Kempe, a soft-spoken and gentle man who gets his results by the quietest of means, was chatting after rehearsal to one of the violin players.

'I believe you yourself have done some conducting, Mr Daines?' he said.

'Yes, Dr Kempe,' was the reply.

'And what is it, do you think, that the conductor needs most from the orchestra?'

'Oh, I suppose he needs response.'

'Well, yes,' said Kempe. 'But what he needs all the time is – help!'

*　　*　　*

'Assassins!'
>   *Toscanini expressing displeasure with the Orchestra.*

*   *   *

'I hate shyness in art as much as I approve of it in life.'
>   *Bruno Walter*

*   *   *

Fritz Reiner was conducting on an extensive American tour in which the second half of the concert programmes consisted sometimes of Debussy's *La Mer* and sometimes of Richard Strauss's *Don Juan*.

At one concert a player had got the wrong music and launched into *Don Juan* as the rest of the orchestra started *La Mer*. Afterwards, Reiner called him aside and told him he was fired. The man protested that this was the kind of mistake anyone could make at the end of a long and exhausting tour.

'Oh, it's not that,' said Reiner. 'It's the way you play *Don Juan*.'

*   *   *

Sir Malcolm Sargent served in the Durham Light Infantry in World War I. Years afterwards he was asked what rank he had held. 'No rank,' he said. 'Just one of the file.'

*　　*　　*

Beecham was not keen on having women as members of his orchestra:

'Is there supposed to be a prejudice against women among conductors? I can only suppose that it must be because their presence imposes restrictions upon one's vocabulary at rehearsals.'

'If the lady is well favoured, I do not like to play near her. If she is not, I am afraid I cannot.'

'I once had an orchestra in which there was only one woman, and she played the harp. I found it impossible to conduct a rehearsal efficiently, and I had to get rid of her. She was a danger to the whole season. If she is not a danger, that orchestra is not fit to be called an orchestra! The man who is not thrilled to the bone by the spectacle of a woman playing the flute, blowing a clarinet or struggling with the intricacies of a trombone, is no man.'

*　　*　　*

'We were so cramped that I had to stand on a shelf, strapped to the wall so that I couldn't fall off. While conducting with my right hand, I kept my left hand on the soprano's head, pushing her towards the horn on low notes to "bump" them up and pulling her back from it on high ones to avoid "blast".

'For one of his entries the baritone had to crawl under the violinists' elbows, surface just in front of the horn, bob down and crawl back. We must have looked as funny as any Marx Brothers film. The results sounded remarkably good for all that.'

Sir Malcolm Sargent on the early days of recording

*   *   *

'I couldn't care less about *you*. *I'm* having the time of my life. It's the most wonderful feeling of neurotic power in the world. I think I would rather do this than anything I know. I would travel anywhere in the world to conduct a symphony orchestra. . . . Say, does Malcolm Sargent talk this much?'

Danny Kaye conducting the London Philharmonic Orchestra at the Royal Albert Hall in a concert in aid of the LPO Trust

*   *   *

'He'll drive his musicians to tears, but they love him for it. They know he is right.'

Victor de Sabata on Toscanini

*　　*　　*

Alerto

Singers

'I hope it's not full of my tantrums!'
*Maria Callas, all smiles, arriving
at a party to launch Harold Rosenthal's
book 'Two Centuries of Opera at
Covent Garden'*

* * *

It has been said that, when starting to sing *Che gelida manina* ('Your tiny hand is frozen') in *La Bohème*, Caruso pressed a hot potato (or was it a hot sausage?) into the soprano's hand.

And, so the story goes, he carefully placed a chamber-pot so that, when the bed was moved to receive the dying Mimi in the last act, the utensil was revealed to the audience in all its splendour.

It is certain, however, that in a performance of *Bohème* the bass who was singing Colline whispered that he had suddenly lost his voice and could not sing his big aria, the *Coat Song*. The great tenor told him to move his lips and, turning his back to the audience, sang the bass aria for him!

His colleagues persuaded him to record this novelty

but, after a few copies had been taken, Caruso insisted that the master disc should be destroyed.

'I don't want to spoil the bass business!' he chuckled.

(Many years later, one of the copies was traced and the record issued commercially, with a commentary by Frances Alda, who was in the cast at the time).

*   *   *

'We would like the figures of the singers to be in keeping with the roles they are singing. But personally I would rather have a fat tenor with a satisfying voice than a nice, personable tenor with a poor voice.'

Sir Malcolm Sargent

*   *   *

'Take that woman away and bring me another soprano!'
Sir Thomas Beecham, rehearsing an opera in Buenos Aires

*   *   *

'Composers have been kind to the great tenors. Why don't they give the basses a chance?'

> *Feodor Chaliapin, the great Russian*
> *bass, famed for his interpretation*
> *of the title role in Moussorgsky's*
> *'Boris Godounov'*

* * *

'Good Heavens! You're not Patti. You are asking the fee of a soprano. You're not even a tenor.'

> *Chaliapin's account of the reaction*
> *at Covent Garden when he was first*
> *asked to sing there*

* * *

As a very young man, with little money, Chaliapin was invited to sing at a fashionable dinner. He turned up in borrowed evening dress and brown shoes – blacked over.

But the hostess's pet dog took a fancy to the shoes and started to lick off the blacking. Chaliapin finished up, as he related later, wearing evening dress with brown shoes!

He was generous with his talents but there were times when the demands became just a bit too much. On one occasion, when he had been invited to a dinner, he was asked by a swooping hostess to sing to the guests.

'If you ask me to dinner, you feed me,' said Chaliapin. 'If you ask me to sing, you pay me.'

*   *   *

Leo Slezak, the Czech tenor, was a great one for a bit of fun. On one occasion he caused such a burst of laughter from the chorus when he was appearing as Radames in *Aïda* at the Metropolitan, New York, that they were fined by the management. But Slezak insisted on paying the fine.

In the closing scene of Wagner's *Lohengrin*, Slezak had sung his Farewell and was about to make his departure in the boat drawn by a swan. But, through mistiming, the boat moved away before Slezak could step on board. He glanced at the audience. 'Tell me,' he said, 'what time is the next swan?'

Slezak wrote a book called *Song of Motley: Being the Reminiscences of a Hungry Tenor.*

*   *   *

Rehearsing for a performance of a Delius work, Beecham turned to the members of the BBC Singers and enquired: 'And which of you gentleman is singing the baritone solo?'

A rather shy and reticent baritone replied, 'I'm afraid I am, Sir Thomas.'

'Ah,' said Beecham, 'I trust we do not have to share your apprehension.'

*   *   *

Lotte Lehmann, the famed Marschallin of Richard Strauss's opera, *Der Rosenkavalier*, has for some years directed master-classes in opera in America.

On a visit to London, she was pointing out that, in studying an operatic role, an artist ought not to practise in front of a mirror. By this method, she said, the gestures appeared to have been imposed from outside instead of growing naturally from within. But, she was asked, would there not be difficulty when a producer wished to impose certain gestures and behaviour from outside?

'Oh, yes,' replied Mme Lehmann, with a disarmingly innocent smile. 'I fought with producers all the time!'

But there were subtler methods than fighting:

'I remember once when I was rehearsing a Strauss opera in which I had to fly into a temper. The producer wanted me to rush up and down the stage, waving my arms about. I told him that I could fly into a rage quite nicely sitting down. But no, he would not have that.

'However, I knew that Strauss, who was a very understanding man, would be in the opera-house later in the day. So I waited my time.

'When I was quite sure that Strauss was sitting in front, I said to the producer, innocently, "I wonder if we could do that scene again? I don't think I have got it quite right." He agreed and I exaggerated everything and made it so ridiculous that eventually Strauss said, "My dear, why do you have to rush about like that?"

'In the end, I did it *my* way!'

*   *   *

'Acting is very, very important in opera. But, of course, it is just as well if you also have a voice!'

Tito Gobbi

*   *   *

The Wit of Music

As a youth, the great Italian baritone Tito Gobbi was so talented that he could have made a successful career either as a singer or as a painter. But his father insisted that, in whatever direction his future might lie, he must learn a 'respectable' job. So he studied law and indeed qualified as a barrister, though he never practised.

Of his early days as an opera singer, Gobbi says, 'I sang my first Scarpia in *Tosca* as a very young man and after the performance I took my mother and father out for a celebration dinner. I ordered the wine in an imperious manner, snapping my fingers to demand the attention of the waiter – for all the world like Scarpia. My father leaned over and said, softly, "Come back, Tito. The opera is over." I was very young then!'

*　　*　　*

Birgit Nilsson, the leading Wagnerian soprano of today, is the wife of the owner of a number of hotels in Sweden. She is also a wit.

At the end of Wagner's opera, *Siegfried*, the hero has braved the magic fire and, on the rocky mountain top, has come upon the figure of Brünnhilde, deep in an enchanted sleep from which she can be awakened only by a hero's kiss.

One night Siegfried (Wolfgang Windgassen) was

somewhat shaken when, leaning over and removing the breastplate of the warrior maiden (Nilsson), he was confronted by a notice taken from one of her husband's hotels: 'Do not disturb!'

*   *   *

'One of my husband's hotels is called *Rheingold*. It's the only one in which I have no part!'

Birgit Nilsson

*   *   *

Walter Widdop, the British tenor, used to enjoy telling stories against himself. This one, for instance:

He had sung with great success in an oratorio in the north country and on the following morning was waiting on the station platform for his train back to London.

A stranger came up and asked him if he was Walter Widdop. Walter, delighted and flattered to be recognised, agreed that that was so.

'I thought so,' said the man. 'But I don't blame thee so much. I blame the so-and-so's that sent thee.'

*   *   *

David Ward, the British bass, was singing the part of the Commendatore in a Covent Garden production of Mozart's *Don Giovanni*, in which the title role was sung by the Italian baritone, Cesare Siepi.

When they were about to rehearse the brief sword-fight that takes place at the beginning of the opera, Siepi asked, 'Have you handled a foil before, David?'

'Oh, I've had just the usual bit of training for stage purposes,' said Ward.

They faced up – and immediately Ward's foil flew out of his hand.

'You must hold on to it, you know, David,' said Siepi.

Again they faced up and again Ward's foil somersaulted into the air.

It was only later that Ward learned that Siepi had at one time been on the short list for Italy's Olympic Games fencing team!

*　　*　　*

Some years ago, negotiations were in progress at Covent Garden with the idea of engaging a distinguished and decidedly voluptuous foreign soprano to sing there. She demanded an enormous fee.

'But,' protested the Garden manager of the day, 'all we want her to do is *sing*!'

*　　*　　*

Shortly after Maria Callas had been involved in a squabble with a prominent impresario in America, she appeared in a three-way link-up programme on the radio. The other two in the programme were Sir Thomas Beecham and Victor Borge.

It was not long before Beecham broached the subject: 'Did you, madame, hit him on the head with a bottle of beer?'

'Oh the newspapers have written so much about it,' replied Callas.

'Or was it a bottle of something else, madame?' persisted Beecham.

'I never threw anything at anyone, unfortunately. I wish I had.'

'You never did? Oh, what a lost opportunity!'

'Isn't it terrible? Well, you know, there may be a next time.'

*   *   *

'Before choirs – especially if they have ladies in them – I quail!'

Sir Thomas Beecham

*   *   *

The Wit of Music

At a time when Beecham was complaining that he searched in vain for beauty of tune in the music of today, John Christie, founder of Glyndebourne Festival Opera, declared: 'I am still haunted by the melodic beauty of Benjamin Britten's *Rape of Lucretia*. But I live in simplicity in the country.' And he unearthed a poem from *Punch* of 1843:

> The stage is with servants in livery fill'd,
> Whom Sir Thomas – the master of chorus – has
>   drill'd
> To neatly come in at appropriate places,
> Sopranos and altos and tenors and basses.
> To one who has something of musical skill in her
> Is apportioned a solo announcing the milliner;
> To another, whose singing in tune is assured,
> Is entrusted a separate part of the steward;
> While the rest, who are apt to be now and then out,
> Are only permitted together to shout;
> And thus, if a note may by one be neglected,
> It can't, when they sing all at once, be detected.

John Christie added: 'The trouble nowadays is that everyone wants to be heard, and as for the tune, well – "it can't, when they sing all at once, be detected!" '

*　　*　　*

Lawrence Tibbett, the forthright American baritone, sang the title role in Eugene Goossens' opera *Don Juan de Mañara* at Covent Garden, with the British baritone, Dennis Noble, as his illegitimate son, Don José.

During the rehearsal period, Noble was sitting at a corner table in the Savoy Grill when Tibbett and his wife walked in at the other end of the room.

There was considerable raising of polite eyebrows when Tibbett, spotting Noble, called out in a ringing voice, 'This is a damn fine opera, Denny – I call you a bastard three times in the first act!'

*   *   *

During a tour of the Beecham Opera Company, one of the principal singers asked Sir Thomas if he would go with him to his son's school prize-day. In due course the small boy was presented to Sir Thomas.

'Do you sing, my boy?' asked Sir Thomas.

'No, sir,' replied the lad.

'Ah, I see,' murmured Sir Thomas. 'It runs in the family.'

*   *   *

Ernest Newman, the eminent critic, was almost as enthusiastic about boxing as he was about music (as in their own ways were Toscanini and Beecham).

While doing a spell as guest critic in America, Newman wrote a notice of a performance of *Tosca* at the Metropolitan. Of the scene in the second act, in which Tosca (Maria Jeritza) stabs the evil Scarpia (Antonio Scotti), he wrote:

'It was the roughest *Tosca* within my experience. Never have I seen two characters mix it like this. Other Scarpias allow themselves to be counted out after the first jab from the table knife. Mr Scotti rose at the count of eight and the uppercut with which he was at last put to sleep was a beauty.

'The winner left the ring without a mark. The weights were not given in the programme, but Madame Jeritza had the advantage in reach.'

'Ernest Newman: A Memoir' by Vera Newman

*   *   *

Melba, taking a call at the end of an opera at Covent Garden, contended that the most frenzied shouting was coming from a group of devoted Australians out in front. 'They're shouting "Auntie Nellie, Auntie Nellie!" ', she said.

'I rather think, madame,' said Beecham, 'that what they are shouting is "Martinelli, Martinelli!"'

* * *

The story goes that Caruso, at one time, took a fancy to learning to play the flute. Somebody approached him and offered to record the sound of his playing.

Asked whether he would like to buy the recording, Caruso replied: 'No, thank you – but I'll sell you the flute!'

* * *

'I have given up smoking. What a wrench! I feel at times a furious desire for a cigarette – no, not one cigarette but a dozen at a time – but I am holding out and I am all the better.

'Yet I dream, when my singing season is done, of a smoke such as never was. I dream of a monstrous cigar and as I smoke I shall fish. But my singing season never seems to be done, and the little fishes wait – and I can't come to them.'

Feodor Chaliapin

* * *

The Wit of Music

While rehearsing for a performance of *Messiah*, Beecham stopped the proceedings and addressed the choir:

'When we sing, "All we like sheep have gone astray", might we, please, have a little more regret and a little less satisfaction?'

Composers

ON ARRIVAL on a visit to the United States, Ralph Vaughan Williams was met by a crowd of reporters.

One of them seized him by the arm and said, 'Tell me, Dr Vaughan Williams, what do you think about music?'

The old man peered quizzically into his face and made the solemn pronouncement: 'It's a Rum Go!'

*   *   *

'Of course there are splendid things in Wagner. But he would go on so. He needed a good sub-editor.'

Constant Lambert

*   *   *

'If an opera cannot be played by an organ-grinder, as Puccini's and Verdi's melodies were played, then that opera is not going to achieve immortality.'

Sir Thomas Beecham

*   *   *

Mascagni came over to London soon after his *Cavalleria Rusticana* had brought him great success. He was staying at the old Metropole Hotel and outside his window an Italian organ-grinder used to play the intermezzo from the opera. But he always played it too fast. One morning Mascagni could stand it no longer. He went down and told the man he must play it more slowly. Next day Mascagni saw that the man was carrying a placard over his barrel-organ: 'Peppino, pupil of Mascagni'.

*   *   *

George Gershwin was a brilliant natural musician but in his earlier days he did not know how to 'write the dots'. His *Rhapsody in Blue*, for instance, was orchestrated for him by Ferdinand Grofé. But he was determined to learn the technique of writing for the orchestra and he went to several people for lessons, among them Stravinsky. It was at the time when Gershwin's music for films and the theatre – orchestrated by others – was making him large sums of money.

'They tell me,' said Stravinsky, 'that you earn a million dollars a year.'

'Oh,' said Gershwin, 'these things are always exaggerated. It's only about half that.'

'Even so,' said Stravinsky, 'will *you* give *me* lessons?'

*   *   *

Not so long ago it was suggested to Stravinsky that he charged very high fees for his appearances and for the performance of his works. 'I do it,' he said. 'on behalf of my brother composers, Schubert and Mozart, who died in poverty.'

*   *   *

After Stravinsky had written *Scènes de Ballet* for the Broadway production *Seven Lively Arts*, impresario Billy Rose sent him a wire:

> YOUR MUSIC GREAT SUCCESS COULD BE SENSATIONAL SUCCESS IF YOU WOULD AUTHORISE ROBERT RUSSELL BENNETT RETOUCH ORCHESTRATION STOP BENNETT ORCHESTRATES EVEN THE WORKS OF COLE PORTER.

Stravinsky wired back: SATISFIED WITH GREAT SUCCESS.

*   *   *

'The schweinerei said I imitated Mozart. Imitated! To Hell! I *stole* Mozart!'

> *Igor Stravinsky on his 'neo-classical' period*

*   *   *

The Wit of Music

Mrs Vera Newman, widow of critic Ernest Newman, tells a Stravinsky story: 'It was a lovely party. Stravinsky was one of the guests and he sat next to me at dinner. He caused a good deal of amusement when he took my hand and, beginning at the tips of the fingers, he kissed my hand and arm.

'Suddenly, having arrived nearly at the elbow, he dropped my arm as though it were red-hot, and said: "Oh, I forgot, your husband doesn't like my music!" '

'Ernest Newman: A Memoir' by Vera Newman

*   *   *

When the German composer Max Reger was visiting London, Sir Henry Wood invited him to lunch at his home in Elsworthy Road, Hampstead:

'Knowing nothing in the way of his likes and dislikes, I took the precaution of ringing up the German Club. They told me I must order at least a couple of dozen bottles of beer.

'Never shall I forget the appearance of our dining-room with all these bottles in a row. The lunch began at one – as lunches did in those days – but it did not end until half-past three when we retired to the drawing-room. Although the good Reger had lived up to his reputation and had consumed most of the beer without the slightest

---

inconvenience to himself, I though the poor fellow might be thirsty so I offered him a whisky and soda. He was so pleased with the first that he had three more. He did not, however, remain to tea. He drove down to the German Club after leaving us. I told Olga I thought he had gone down there to get a drink.'

'*My Life of Music*' *by Henry J. Wood*

*　　*　　*

'I quite enjoyed being hissed – it made a change.'

Sir William Walton after a performance of his opera 'Troilus and Cressida' had received a mixed reception in Italy

*　　*　　*

'If a man accepts applause when people like what he does, he should be man enough to accept hissing from people who don't like it.'

Leopold Stokowski

*　　*　　*

While Beecham was rehearsing a new work by Frederick Delius in Queen's Hall, the composer was sitting up in the circle.

'Was that all right, Fred?' Beecham called out into space.

'Yes, except for the horns, perhaps,' came back the voice of Delius.

'Gentlemen, we'll try from bar X again.' ...

'Yes, that was all right,' called out Delius.

'Oh, good,' said Sir Thomas. 'You know there are no horns in that passage.'

* * *

Richard Strauss laughed incredulously when Beecham said he proposed to conduct the first London performance of *Elektra* without a score.

'I'll bet you one hundred pounds I will learn it in a fortnight,' said Beecham.

He did so, but Strauss went back to the Continent without settling the bet. When the time came for payment of the composer's royalties, there was a deduction from the total: 'To one bet, £100.'

* * *

'Not only did he have ideas – he had twenty children. That is achievement.'

Stokowski on Johann Sebastian Bach

*　　*　　*

From sketches left by the composer, the British music-ologist Deryck Cooke prepared a performing version of Mahler's *Symphony No 10*.

When I met Cooke at a party to launch the Promenade Concerts season in which the work was to have its first performance at the Royal Albert Hall, I noticed that he had given himself a cut on the chin while shaving.

'Has the ghost of Mahler been savaging you?' I asked.

'I confess that while puzzling over various points in the music one was tempted to try to conjure up the spirit of Mahler to ask him about his exact intentions,' said Cooke, 'but I never did so. I didn't want to risk his saying, "Take your so-and-so hands off that!"'

(As a matter of fact, Cooke did such an admirable job that his work was very warmly acclaimed.)

*　　*　　*

During a long telephone conversation with Neville
Cardus, Beecham was discoursing upon British composers
from Purcell onwards.

'But what about Elgar?' asked Cardus.

'What about him?' said Sir Thomas. 'Isn't he well?'

'*You just wait! Some day **I'll** finish first.*'

Instrumentalists

I DON'T KNOW what a great violinist ought to look like – something on Paganini lines, with flowing hair and a haggard, haunted expression, perhaps?

I do know that the amiable and fluent Isaac Stern, though intense and purposeful when involved in a serious discussion, rather suggests a travelling salesman of the best type – until he tucks his violin under his chin. And, come to think of it, I suppose he is a travelling salesman – one of today's most persuasive salesmen of the art of music.

Isaac Stern was born in Russia but taken to the United States at the age of two – and, by the way, it is interesting to note how many of the leading violinists of today are Russian in origin. David Oistrakh and Leonid Kogan are Russian; Jascha Heifetz, Nathan Milstein and Mischa Elman were born in Russia; and Yehudi Menuhin, born in America, had Russian parents.

Stern has a most agile mind, quick on the uptake and ready with brisk repartee when the occasion calls for it. On one of his visits to London he was discussing the European and American musical traditions.

'People in Europe,' he said, 'don't seem to understand the American musical tradition. You ought to realise that the American musical tradition is based on a lot of crewcut gum-chewers like Arturo Toscanini, Bruno Walter, Pierre Monteux and the rest of them.'

He sums up his distinguished career in very few words: 'I do play the violin but not well enough to hold a steady job – just a series of one-night stands.'

Another of Isaac Stern's witticisms: 'If nobody wants to come to your concert, nothing will stop them!'

*   *   *

'You are there – and I am here – but where is Beethoven?'
Artur Schnabel during a piano concerto
rehearsal in which he was not seeing eye
eye to with the conductor

*   *   *

'I regret not being a married man. Nevertheless, I have two children – my Stradivari and my Guarneri.'
Henryk Szeryng

*   *   *

One hears two versions, both of them highly evocative, of Beecham's impression of the characteristic sound of the harpsichord.

The first is: 'Playing a birdcage with a toasting-fork.'

The somewhat racier version is: 'Two skeletons copulating on a galvanised tin roof.'

* * *

'Ashkenazy is small, but the grand piano is not too big for him. He does what he wants with it. Others who are big come to the piano but it is too big for them.'

Emil Gilels on the young Russian pianist Vladimir Ashkenazy

* * *

A manufacturer tried to get Artur Schnabel interested in a mechanical piano which, he pointed out, had been brought to such a stage of perfection that it had sixteen nuances at its disposal.

'Indeed?' commented Schnabel. 'But my playing requires seventeen.'

* * *

Sir Thomas Beecham was the conductor in a performance of a piano concerto in which the solo part was very indifferently played. When the concert was over and the audience had left the hall, he happened to be on the platform when the men in overalls arrived to push off the piano. Sir Thomas strolled over to them.

'I do not think you need trouble yourselves, gentlemen,' he said. 'Just give the instrument a little time in which to recover and it will slink away of its own accord.'

*   *   *

'What do you have to know to play the cymbals?' someone asked Sir Malcolm Sargent. 'Nothing,' was the reply. 'Just when.'

*   *   *

'Have I a secret about playing the piano? It is a very simple one. I sit down on the piano-stool and make myself comfortable – and I always make sure that the lid over the keyboard is open before I start to play.'

Artur Schnabel

*   *   *

'The pianist cannot afford to be so public-spirited as the famous conductor who, on being accused of having drowned the singers with his orchestra, replied: "I know, I did it intentionally, and thought that by doing so I had done a public service."'

Gerald Moore

*   *   *

Fritz Kreisler was strolling with a friend in a New York street when they happened to pass a fish shop. He waved a hand towards the rows of protruding eyes and gaping mouths on the slab.

'Ah,' he said. 'That reminds me – I have a concert tonight!'

*   *   *

A famous string quartet visited a north-country town and gave a highly successful concert. Afterwards the local mayor made a speech in which he said, 'They might think we don't know much about culture up 'ere. But we do. We've enjoyed your concert and we 'ope you'll come back. And we 'ope that next time you'll bring t'full band.'

*   *   *

The Wit of Music

When José Iturbi first came to England many years ago, he did not speak the English language at all. He wanted a cup of tea but the situation became involved and he was offered almost everything else. But he solved the problem by sitting down at the piano and playing, *Tea for Two*. He got his cup of tea.

Conductor as well as pianist, Iturbi brought the Valencia Municipal Orchestra to England on tour some fifteen years ago.

'In an hour,' he bewailed, 'I've been asked twenty times to play the *Harry Lime Theme*. I've never heard of it.'

'You can arrange for a picnic with hamburger, but when you have a stiff-shirt-and-white-tie dinner, you serve caviar. It's the same with music. Boogie-woogie for picnics: Beethoven for white tie.'

José Iturbi

* * *

Albert Einstein, a very keen violinist, often played violin-and-piano sonatas with Artur Schnabel. After trying one passage several times, Einstein was still having difficulty in co-ordinating violin with piano.

'My dear Albert,' said Schnabel. 'Can't you count?'

(This story is told also of another Artur – Artur Rubinstein. You must take your choice).

*   *   *

Few artists have done as much as Gerald Moore in establishing the proper status of accompanists – he cheerfully calls himself the 'unashamed' accompanist. Gone are the days when it was considered sufficient for the pianist to 'assist at the piano' – 'discreetly' of course. The piano is an integral part in the performance of fine songs and Gerald Moore has for years been the chosen partner of many of the greatest singers.

On one occasion years ago, Moore agreed to accompany at Wigmore Hall a soprano who at once showed that she knew little or nothing about the art of singing. She received only one Press notice – and that was a very bad one.

Some time later she met Moore again and insisted that it was because she was Australian that the critics had been so unkind.

Moore would have none of that and pointed out that, on the contrary, Australian singers were very popular in Britain.

But she perisisted in her belief. 'It's because of the body-line bowling, you know,' she said.

*   *   *

'Most unfortunate results will attend the accompanist who does not know what he is playing about – what the singer is singing about. A young friend of mine was playing the accompaniment to me one day of Wolf's song 'Bitt ihn, O Mutter' ('Beg him, O Mother'). This accompaniment is written with Wolf's usual eloquence and urgency, but it was played by this young lady with such viciousness that I ventured to ask her if she knew what 'Bitt ihn, O Mutter' meant. 'Of course.' she replied. 'It means "O Mother, bite him!" '

Gerald Moore

*　　　*　　　*

Not feeling well, Pablo Casals was attended by a distinguished heart specialist.

'Ah,' he said when he saw the doctor, 'you are the doctor who attended President Eisenhower. You are a very famous man.'

'But,' said the doctor, modestly, 'I'll never be as famous as you are.'

'Yes,' said Casals, thoughtfully. 'That's true.'

*　　　*　　　*

In his younger days, Jascha Heifetz was a crack table-tennis player. But fellow violinist Nathan Milstein proudly boasted that he once beat him.

'And what's more,' declared Milstein, 'I beat him after I had played the Mendelssohn *Violin Concerto* under Toscanini!'

* * *

Moiseiwitsch was a close personal friend of Rachmaninov and one of the finest exponents of his piano works. He used to tell how Rachmaninov had great difficulty in playing one particular variation in his own *Rhapsody on a Theme of Paganini* for piano and orchestra.

One evening at dinner, though Rachmaninov protested that he was a non-drinker, Benno persuaded him to have a glass of *crème-de-menthe*, with the assurance that he would have no worries about that variation. Sure enough, this was so – and ever afterwards Rachmaninov had a glass of *crème-de-menthe* before playing that work.

'It became known as the *Crème-de-Menthe Variation*,' said Benno.

* * *

The Wit of Music

Though a man of abounding wit, Benno Moiseiwitsch had the immobile face of the good poker-player that he was. The cover of an old dinner menu in the Savage Club is ringed with musical terms expressive of various emotions. Over each is the face of Moiseiwitsch – wearing exactly the same expression!

One of his close friends was his fellow pianist Mark Hambourg, often his companion at the card table in the Savage.

Mark, who had rather a Beethoven-type head, arrived at the club one day full of enthusiasm.

'Benno,' he said. 'A wonderful thing has happened. They are going to make a film about the life of Beethoven – and they have asked me to play Beethoven.'

'Splendid, Mark,' said Benno. 'Who's going to play the piano?'

One evening at cards Hambourg complained that the light was so bad that it was difficult to see the cards.

'Surely by now, Mark,' said Benno, 'you can play by memory!'

In the Savage one evening a club bore launched upon a tedious and badly told story. Eventually the tale ground to its conclusion.

'Ah, yes,' murmured the impassive Moiseiwitsch. 'I remember – some years ago I heard a humorous version of that.'

*　　*　　*

Jascha Heifetz and Mischa Elman were sitting together at a dinner when a note was handed up. It was addressed, so the story goes, 'To the Greatest Violinist in the World'.

'You'd better open it, Mischa,' said Heifetz.

'No, no,' said Elman. 'You open it, Jascha.'

They agreed to open it together. It began, 'Dear Fritz . . .'

Audiences

WHAT IS IT that Tchaikovsky in the concert hall does to people who are, I suppose, normal decent citizens? Perhaps it is the same kind of thing that the motor-car does to some other normal decent citizens – makes them anti-social.

Take, for instance, the *Symphony No 5* at the Royal Festival Hall.

In the terrace-stall in front of me was a man I learned to hate. He conducted every nuance of the music, nodding with approval only when Antal Dorati and the London Symphony Orchestra seemed to be more or less with him. He had a high old time – and gave me hell.

The girl across the gangway was not too bad, though an ostentatious programme-tapper. But in front of her was not so much a conductor as a thrower-abouter. One moment he would writhe and crouch in his seat and the next would be plunging from side to side, gnawing his knuckles. Clearly he was being 'sent'.

Perhaps it was an unusually strange audience – strange enough, at any rate, for a section to burst in with hearty applause some little time before Tchaikovsky had finished his say.

Leslie Ayre
The Evening News, London

*　　*　　*

It does seem that there is a good deal more 'audience participation' in American concert halls:

'Painters paint on canvas,' conductor Leopold Stokowski once lectured an unruly audience. 'We paint our tone picture on silence. Only you can supply that.'

But they never do. In fact, when the house lights go down on a concert today, it is often the audience that strikes up the overture. It is a kind of barnyard symphonette. The Hummer and the Time Beater serve as the rhythm section; the Cellophane Crinkler and the Programme Rattler handle the solos. In the percussion section, the principal performers are the Bracelet Jangler and the Premature Clapper, while special effects are contributed by the Knuckle Cracker and the Watch Winder. The Coughers' Chorale is directed by the Dry-throated Red-nosed Hacker, whose feeblest lead always gets a resounding antiphonal response. The entire performance is choreographed by Fidgeter, produced and upstaged by that notorious team of Latecomer and Earlyleaver.

Courtesy Time
Copyright Time Inc 1966

*   *   *

One of the most sensational clashes between performer and audience occurred during a performance of *Fidelio*, conducted by Sir Thomas Beecham at Covent Garden.

The overture had not been long in progress when Beecham was impelled to shout 'Stop talking!' at the audience and, later in the evening, premature applause drew forth a frenzied 'Shut up, you!' from him.

Recalling the incident some years later, he said: 'The audiences at the opera are improving. They only talk quite casually during the performance and if you turn round and shout at them they are quiet.

'Of course you can have too much silence. Once at Covent Garden I turned round during *Fidelio* and told the gallery to shut up because of their intrusive applause. After that they didn't applaud anything for months. You could hear aitches dropped. The silence spread to the concert hall. One night I mounted the rostrum and said: "Ladies and gentlemen, let us pray."'

*   *   *

'Occasionally I look round at a concert and see row upon row of faces. They are anything but inspiring. They tend to put one off. Give me an empty gramophone studio to play in!'

Sir Thomas Beecham

*   *   *

On the question of evening dress, Beecham expressed somewhat contradictory views: 'I believe that on all public occasions everyone should dress up to the nines. If I dress for a concert, why can't the audience dress, too? It is a very one-sided business. Alas, nowadays in our country, the ladies seldom if ever dress up. It is their fault. It is not the fault of the men. If the women would only break the ice and put on their gladdest of glad-rags, with tiaras, glittering jewels and fans, the men would give in. Then the glories of the concert hall would return.'

'I don't care whether they come dressed by Schiaparelli or in woad, so long as they come.'

*　　　*　　　*

'Every three or four minutes some fascinating young female fell into the fountain and had to be rescued by a chivalrous swain. It must have happened thirty-five times every night. Foreigners came from all parts of Europe to see it.'

> *Beecham's description of the audiences*
> *in the early days of the Promenade*
> *Concerts at Queen's Hall*

*　　　*　　　*

The Royal Festival Hall, proud of its sensitive acoustics, includes a note in every programme, begging the audience to refrain from coughing. At one recital by the Russian pianist, Sviatoslav Richter, however, there was a great deal of sporadic coughing. A few nights later, this piece of advice appeared in the programme:

'There are two ways of coping with a cough during a concert. One is to suppress it entirely – as the artists invariably manage to do during performances. The second way – when complete suppression is not possible – is to muffle the cough by the discreet use of the hand-kerchief.

'There is a third way, but since this is distracting to both the artist and the audience, it is unlikely to find favour with Festival Hall patrons. It is to open the mouth and use it as a sounding-board for projecting the cough into every part of the auditorium. A single unrestrained cough of this character, released during a quiet passage of music, can effectively ruin the enjoyment of three thousand listeners, on whose behalf this homily is published.'

*   *   *

'A "lollipop" in accepted English terminology is a species of sweetmeat or candy. I have used the word in connection with music played by me in my concerts for the following reasons. For many years past my audience at the close of a performance has had the disconcerting habit of remaining in its seat and declining to depart until, emulating Oliver Twist, it has obtained an extra helping.

'As in the majority of cases the programme ends with a grand bang or explosion of sound, my practice has been to play an encore which is in complete contrast. The piece selected has generally been of an essentially syrupy, soapy, soothing and even soporific nature and the effect upon the audience has been that its emotional temperature, raised to a high point at the conclusion of the actual programme, is gradually reduced to the normal, so that everyone walks out happy and comfortable.

'The idea is not wholly original, for it is to be found in the old Athenian drama, where tragedies were followed by satirical comedies or other forms of fooling. Of course, when, as in the case of a symphony such as the *Sixth* of Tchaikovsky, there is a quiet ending, the character of the "lollipop" suffers a slight change and the former "tranquilliser" is replaced by something of a more genial type. But in every case these little epilogues, corollaries or afterthoughts are short, taking and popular in style. In other words, a musical sweetmeat or, to make use of transatlantic idiom – a candy.'

Sir Thomas Beecham

*   *   *

The Wit of Music

Audiences at Glyndebourne Festival Opera are, of course, somewhat unusually constituted. Some are there as opera-lovers, some are there to admire the beautiful grounds (weather permitting) – and some are there because it is very much the socially 'done thing'. Indeed, the Glyndebourne 'regulars' make quite a hobby of collecting the more bizarre comments on the opera.

After the première of *Elegy for Young Lovers* by the very 'modern' composer, Heinz Werner Henze:

'Who was the composer of tonight's opera?'

'It's always Mozart here.'

'Really – he must have been very young – before he learned to write those pretty tunes.'

And after Gluck's *Orfeo*:

'All I can say is it didn't sound much like Offenbach to me!'

*　　　*　　　*

But one must not forget the lady at the Metropolitan, who leaned over and whispered to the conductor: 'I wonder if you could play the third act before the second tonight? My friend and I have to catch a train and we do so want to know how it all ends.'

Sir Thomas

'I AM A peaceful and harmless man, I can't understand why people are always going for me.'

* * *

'English is a terrible language for vocalising. Try singing Love or Death. But, ah! – Liebe, Amore, Tod!

* * *

During a break in rehearsal, a photographer asked Sir Thomas if he could appear to be conducting while a picture was taken.

'My dear fellow,' said Sir Thomas. 'I never *appear* to be conducting. Either I conduct or I do not conduct.'

* * *

At the Edinburgh Festival:

'Festivals are for the purpose of attracting trade to the town. What that has to do with music, I don't know.'

* * *

'Who has written a single outstanding melody in the last forty years? Who has written a melody that people will whistle or sing? You remember Rossini's asking a young man who brought him some music, "Do you think it is going to grind?"'

*　　　*　　　*

After an accident Beecham arrived at a meeting leaning heavily on two sticks:

'I am obliged to arrive in this way and I shall be obliged to go off in precisely the same way. I am in this curious situation: I can lie down, I can stand up, but I cannot sit down. I have not experienced this curious sensation since the days when I was a small boy at school.'

*　　　*　　　*

'Why do we have to have all these third-rate foreign conductors around – when we have so many second-rate ones of our own?'

*　　　*　　　*

When Beecham was visiting Liverpool with his company, he pointed out to the manager of the theatre that, as one of the operas called for a very large orchestra, he would be taking over two of the boxes to accommodate the overflow of the players. The manager protested that these boxes had already been sold.

'In that case,' said Sir Thomas, 'you will just have to tell them to drop in next time we are in town.'

*   *   *

Things seemed to Sir Thomas to be going lethargically and without the necessary passion during a rehearsal of *Tristan and Isolde*.

'Ladies and gentlemen,' he protested, 'we are engaged upon the great love drama of *Tristan and Isolde* – not Darby and Joan!'

*   *   *

'My father was one of the first men to buy an electrical organ. The first time I played it, one night in November, I put out all the lights in St Helens.'

*   *   *

The Wit of Music

When told that an eight-year-old Italian boy had gone to the United States to conduct orchestras, Sir Thomas declared:

'Who is responsible for this outrage? The child should be in a kindergarten, sucking a lollipop. But I did once know an orang-outang who would open the door, put you to bed and then play the piano for you.'

* * *

Sir Thomas, who had conducted the ship's orchestra during a voyage to Capetown, was asked what he thought of it.

'Wait till I get ashore first,' he said.

* * *

When Beecham was in America, his friend Sir Beverley Baxter, MP, sent him a telegram: WHY DON'T YOU COME HOME? ENGLAND HATH NEED OF THEE.

Sir Thomas wired back: WHY DON'T YOU COME HERE? 'THE METROPOLITAN' NEEDS A SINGING POLITICIAN.

* * *

'It takes the English musical public thirty-five to forty years to get the name of a piece – sixty to seventy to decide they want to hear it.'

*   *   *

'This is the only country in the world where musicians are not expected to live. Of course, composers and musicians have always starved and, as this is a sentimental country, we think the tradition should be continued.'

*   *   *

'In my youth there were stacks of ditties about love and moonlight on every pianoforte. One of the purveyors of this nonsense made a handsome fortune out of it. He wrote five thousand of these lyrics – all set to music, all sung for thirty or forty years by every young female acquiring a musical education. Think of the mental and moral disintegration that must have gone on in the soul of that young woman by singing those five thousand specimens of rubbish!'

*   *   *   73

The Wit of Music

Just before World War II began, Beecham had announced a period of retirement. But he changed his mind and continued to conduct.

'We were given to understand that the country was in a state of emergency,' he said. 'So I emerged.'

*   *   *

'In spite of our little difficulties and troubles, we are really a very happy family at Covent Garden. We always meet in the morning on the best of terms. By two o'clock in the afternoon we are ready to cut each other's throats. By the middle of the evening performance ancient friendships have been broken and family ties sundered, and at the end of the day, people part, never to meet again. But at ten o'clock the next morning all is forgiven and forgotten, and we start our daily round once more.

'That, I am sure you will all agree, is the ideal state of things. How can you compare it with the flat level of monotonous existence! Happiness is impossible without continual bickering and friction. Such things are vital to human happiness.'

*   *   *

Sir Thomas appeared at the Dome, Brighton, shortly after it had been opened. Later, he had this to say:

'So someone at Brighton says I insulted the place by not playing *God Save the King*? Well, we did play it. That is enough. For Brighton it is more than enough.

'I have been asked for my opinion of the Dome, and I am going to pass it on. The first thing I have to grumble about is the heat. The dressing-rooms are up three flights of stairs and they have all been hermetically sealed. They all have windows but none of them will open. I have put my stick through three of them and I intend to put my stick through the rest of them before I go.

'I am waiting for the day when some fat prima donna comes to the Dome and has to climb up those three flights of stairs. She will go up and never come down again. I wonder what those old warhorses of song, Melba and Tetrazzini, would have said!

'I congratulate you on this magnificent building and I hope you will find a use for it.

(*Sir Thomas confessed later that he had been* 'speaking metaphorically' *in his reference to broken windows.*)

*   *   *

'The BBC is a monopolistic piece of lunacy.'

*   *   *

The Wit of Music

At a time when he was involved in the making of a film about the life of Mozart:

'My one regret is that more of the music of Mozart has not been included in the film, although I am given what are alleged to be excellent reasons why, in the life of the world's greatest composer, so little of his music should be heard. I am further given to understand that this apparent discrepancy or paradox is entirely characteristic of film management and outlook. I look forward some day to seeing a film on the life of Shakespeare which will not contain one single literary reference to the work of the Bard.'

*   *   *

'I hear you have been staying down at Lord So-and-So's?' a friend said to Beecham.

'Yes,' replied Sir Thomas, 'I spent a month down there last weekend.'

*   *   *

'The BBC is not, never was and, I sincerely hope, never will be more than a vast bureau of popular entertainment.'

*   *   *

Asked what he proposed to do at the end of the opera season, Beecham replied:

'I propose to go shooting – shooting anyone who mentions music.'

*　　*　　*

'We are a hundred years behind everybody else – which is not so bad as the Americans, who are two hundred years behind. After the Americans, however, we are the laggards in culture.'

*　　*　　*

'I am seriously beginning to think that the British public is not made for education. It would be better to leave it alone in its raw condition of intelligent ignorance. Its poor brain is obviously bewildered by the mass of rubbish that our professional music teachers have endeavoured to insert therein. I do not see the slightest chance of success for novelties here, and the public will be content with a tedious and sordid round of *Butterflies*, *Carmens* and *Bohemian Girls*.'

*　　*　　*

'I find brass bands have a melancholy sound – yes, melancholy. All right out of doors, of course – fifty miles
away. Like bagpipes, they turn what had been a dream
into a public nuisance.'

*   *   *

Sir Thomas turned up in London from Paris one day,
sporting a severely sprained wrist.

'Never,' he advised, 'never try to climb the Eiffel
Tower!'

*   *   *

'Unfortunately, so long as our MPs are drawn from the
more ignorant section of the community, I see little hope
of improvement. The only chance for music that I see
is that in the course of time a different breed of politician
may spring up with some glimmering of artistic intelli-
gence.'

*   *   *

Interrupting a rehearsal:

'Gentlemen, I understand that there is someone to see me from the Official Receiver's Office. For what he is about to receive may the Lord make him truly thankful.'

*   *   *

On missed cues at rehearsal:

'That young man over there – he's immaculately dressed. His tie is right, his shoes are polished and his hair well brushed. But I do wish he would play something.'

'It seems to be asking too much for you to be with us all the time, sir, but perhaps you would be so good as to keep in touch now and then.'

'You play very beautifully, my dear fellow, but do you think you might play more frequently?'

*   *   *

'I have never been rude about the BBC.'

*   *   *

The Wit of Music

There *were* occasions when Sir Thomas met his match. On arrival in a provincial town, he found that his favourite suite of rooms was occupied by a businessman, whom the manager could not persuade to move. During a discussion in the foyer, Beecham said: 'Do you know who I am? I am Sir Thomas Beecham.'

'My dear chap,' said the other, 'even if you were Billy Cotton I wouldn't change my rooms!'

*   *   *

'I hate television. It does nothing for music. I once saw an opera singer on television. That is to say that I saw a close-up of the whole contents of her throat – tonsils, adenoids everything practically down to her stomach. Some people may call that entertainment. I do not.'

*   *   *

'Broadcasting is the foremost misfortune that has ever overtaken this planet.'

*   *   *

'We hear about this brain-washing today, a process whereby you come out a different person afterwards. Well, we have all had our brains washed. We have no standards whatever. We are the most ignorant public in the world and we have more music than ever, too much music. The BBC are plugging away every day with all this awful stuff.'

*   *   *

Arriving to start a tour of Australia, in 1940, Sir Thomas made this pronouncement:

'This is my farewell tour, but I shall repeat it regularly for the next thirty years. The more you emphasise that this definitely is your farewell, the oftener you repeat it. These tours are like politicians. They were with us in 1915 and they are still with us.'

*   *   *

'I make good resolutions every day – and always break them by the evening.'

*   *   *

At a birthday dinner for Beecham, the chairman read congratulatory telegrams from leading figures in music all over the world. There was tremendous applause and, when it had died away, Beecham took his cigar from his mouth and enquired in a tone of mild disappointment:

'Nothing from Mozart?'

Five years later, at a luncheon to celebrate his eightieth birthday, he had this to say:

'As a young man I took to acknowledging all the applause that was going. One day I heard an elderly gentleman of military appearance say to his wife, "My dear, look at him – bowing all the time. He doesn't do the work." It came as real surprise to me. In the next ten years I came to the conclusion he was right. Since then I have never done any work at all.'

* * *

'On occasions, the leaders of famous orchestras on either side of the Atlantic have said to me, "Thank you very much, sir. I speak for the whole orchestra." "What have I done?" I have asked. "You have let us play." '

* * *

'I assure you that hardly ever do I interfere with them. The role of the conductor is grossly mistaken. His duty is not to interfere with the orchestra. When I am rehearsing, I say, "We'll play the whole thing through from beginning to end. You will probably make some mistakes." Then they play it twice and make no mistakes. I say, "That is absolute perfection. We shall meet on the night of the concert – then I'll decide what I'm going to do." '

*　　*　　*

'There are only two things to remember – you begin together – and you end together. What you do in between doesn't matter. The audience won't know, anyway. That is the Golden Rule.'

*　　*　　*

'The Press sometimes refer to me as the Greatest English Conductor. I will not be called the Greatest English Conductor . . . but I do know that I am a damned sight better than any foreigner.'

*　　*　　*

'I shall now proceed to enter an era in which I shall make myself more objectionable than I have ever done – but in a very pleasant way. It is possible to do most awful things in the sweetest way. Age is nothing. Years are nothing. All that matters is thought and feeling.

'If you are satisfied that what you are doing at the moment is right – even if it is wrong – that is all that matters. That is all that matters in art. Whether you are singing or playing or conducting – or misconducting – do it with conviction!'

Maestoso

'Lollipops'

IN THESE DAYS, the idea of heavyweight sopranos and two-ton tenors seems a thing of the past. Operatic singers nowadays usually contrive to look presentable and even credible in their romantic roles. Yet one cannot help feeling a tinge of regret at not having encountered in the flesh – the considerable flesh – the monumental singers and other impressive figures who have populated Beachcomber's world of music in the *Daily Express*:

'I wrote recently of cases of sabotage among orchestras. There had been an interval at a concert while a clarinet-player mended his instrument. And I have just read that the pin-support fell off a 'cello at another concert. Who is behind the concert-hall gangs? Players are finding "Down with music!" chalked on drums. Trombones are being filled with dirty water. Tin-tacks are stuck in oboes. Three violinists cut their chins on the jagged edges of their instruments. The Guatemalan pianist, Yppippooray, on sitting down to play Scarpini's *Ravanello*, had scarcely struck the first note when steam poured out of his instrument.

' "Are you sure it's all right?" whispered an impresario in the wings.

' "Oh, rather. It's only steam," said an Abominable Yesman.'

The Wit of Music

'I read that Caruso once pressed a hot sausage into Melba's hand while he was singing *Your tiny hand is frozen*. If he had had the nerve to continue, "Let me warm it with a sausage", he would have made operatic history. Broccoli, on a similar occasion, after a glance at the massive paw of Rustiguzzi, sang, "Your enormous hand is frozen", not as a joke, but from absent-mindedness. At Covent Garden three years ago, when Rustiguzzi was in full spate and had roared twice in *Mirandola*, "I implore you! I implore you", Scampi muttered under his breath, "I heard you the first time".'

'It needs considerable courage and genuine love of music to go on singing after you have swallowed your false moustache. This happened to a tenor in *Rigoletto* the other day, at Covent Garden. The worst tumble-cum-trivy I can recall was at the Opéra in Paris during a performance of *Catrina*. Gaillard's beard became entangled in Mme Adénoïde's wig during the great duet in Act II. A spearman tried to disentangle it, but the point of the spear got caught like a knitting needle, and the shaft jammed between Gaillard's legs. He lost his balance and banged not only his head but hers against a castle wall. A peasant sitting on the wall was dislodged and got her right arm stuck in the mass of beard and wig. After a kind of Rugger scrum, during which the four of them rolled round the stage, the curtain was rung down.'

'There is no doubt that we are a musical nation. Not for a long time have I had so many letters, each one enclosing a cutting about the tenor who swallowed his moustache. But I have waited in vain for advertisements saying: "Maxwell's Moustaches go down easiest" or "Galbraith's Moustache-Glue gave Caruso confidence" or "Swallow one of Pimbleton's vanilla-flavoured moustaches". Makers of operatic moustaches are missing a great chance.'

(*In fact, the artist who swallowed his moustache at Covent Garden was the Yorkshire-born tenor Walter Midgley*).

' "Her singing of the aria brought the mouse down." (Music critic.)

'The singer drew back in alarm. "I think I'm going to shriek," she said.

' "You have been shrieking," riposted the mouse. "There's no peace behind the wainscot with this din going on."

' "And what do you know of music?" asked the trembling diva.

' "My father was a singing mouse, trained by a clergyman," was the proud reply.

' "Who was his favourite composer?" queried the soprano.

' "Moussorgsky," vouchsafed the tiny beast.'

Beachcomber, Daily Express

*   *   *

'Singing mice have often been mentioned and exhibited but imposture has commonly been suspected.'

Charles Darwin

*   *   *

Among the wildest extravaganzas were the Hoffnung Festivals organised in London by the artist-musician Gerard Hoffnung, One could never be sure what might happen next – the appearance of such unusual 'instruments' as repeating rifles and electric floor-polishers or a *Piano Concerto To End All Piano Concertos*, with soloist Yvonne Arnaud finishing up by throwing her knitting at the conductor. Or it might be the great horn-player, Dennis Brain, appearing as soloist in a *Concerto for Hosepipe and Strings* or a Chopin nocturne arranged for four bass tubas, the biggest of them an eight-foot-high affair mounted on wheels.

One of the most effective musical jokes perpetrated by Hoffnung was heralded by the appearance on the platform of the Royal Festival Hall, of Ernest Bean, then the general manger. He solemnly announced that, though the main spirit of the evening was one of hilarity, the next item would be quite serious. Sir William Walton happened to be in town and had kindly agreed to conduct an excerpt from his famous oratorio, *Belshazzar's Feast*.

Cheers greeted Sir William as he walked on to the

---

platform with soloist Owen Brannigan and bowed to the audience, the orchestra and the massed chorus.

He raised his baton – and the chorus roared forth the single word from the oratorio: 'Slain!' Then Sir William shook hands with Mr Brannigan, who had not opened his mouth, and with the leader of the orchestra, who had not played a note, bowed to the chorus and to the audience – and departed to tremendous applause.

*   *   *

A foreign conductor became more and more irritated by the talking and whispering among the orchestra during rehearsal. He called for silence several times but was still not satisfied.

Eventually, in a frenzy, he called out: 'I can stand it then and now – but, my God, all the time, never!'

*   *   *

'Mr Blank was one of the last survivors of the band of musicians who formerly occupied the west gallery of the church. In this he for years did double service, simultaneously singing tenor and playing the bassoon.'

Newspaper obituary notice

*   *   *

The Wit of Music

Two dear old Scottish ladies were leaving the theatre after a performance of *Tristan and Isolde* by a visiting German company at the Edinburgh Festival had at last reached its conclusion. They appeared to be in a state of considerable bewilderment, as though they had had no idea of what was in store for them.

During the course of the performance, the burly tenor, Wolfgang Windgassen, had twice crashed spectacularly to the ground in his death struggles as Tristan.

The two ladies were silent for some time. Eventually, one of them asked 'Did you enjoy it, Jeanie?'

'Er . . . oh, yes . . . oh, yes, Mary, I enjoyed it.' answered the other, cautiously.

Another long pause, then, 'Did *you* enjoy it, Mary?' asked Jeanie.

'Oh, yes . . . yes, I enjoyed it,' replied Mary. 'He does take some nasty falls, doesn't he!'

Surely there can have been few odder summings-up of an evening of *Tristan*!

*   *   *

When preparations were afoot for one of the annual gatherings organised by the Gaelic Society of London, the president, the late James McPhee, pointed out that one group of singers would be singing in Gaelic for the first time and that ninety per cent of another group had never seen Scotland.

'But what has all this to do with the English?' he was asked.

'It has everything to do with the English,' he replied, dryly. 'They give the prizes.'

*   *   *

'It is strange that, though they will burst into song on no provocation at all, the Welsh have produced so few eminent composers – with, of course, the exception of Johann Sebastian, Bach.'

Anon

*   *   *

Liberace's reaction to adverse criticism: 'I cry all the way to the bank.'

*   *   *

'It has sometimes been said that I don't sing very well. But where would I be if I did!'

Maurice Chevalier

*   *   *

The Wit of Music

A pianist, who was also a keen golfer, was giving a recital in London.

Two fellow pianists met. 'I hear So-and-so is playing Beethoven tonight,' said one.

'Oh, is he?' said the other. 'I'm afraid Beethoven is going to lose.'

*   *   *

'When I practise the piano my four-month-old white budgerigar, Blanco, sits on a tiny stool at an eighteenth-century enamel and gilt grand piano only four and a half inches long and taps it with his beak. Snowy, an older bird, sits on the music-rest and sways to the music.'

Letter to a newspaper

*   *   *

When Sam Goldwyn was planning a mighty film spectacle, he announced, 'I don't want one composer to do the music – I want six. I want something like Wagner – but louder!'

*   *   *

'Lollipops'

'Piano (overstrung) for sale by parents (ditto) of heavy-handed daughter.'

Advertisement in a Basingstoke shop window

* * *

'The English may not like music – but they absolutely *love* the noise it makes.'

Sir Thomas Beecham

* * *

'I hate music – especially when it's played.'

Schnozzle Durante

Acknowledgements

It is impossible to discover the sources of some of the stories that circulate among musicians. But I am grateful to friends who have told me stories or have jogged the memory about others.

My specific thanks are due to Mr Tito Gobbi; Victor Gollancz Limited (*My Life of Music* by Henry J Wood); G P Putnam's Sons (*Ernest Newman: A Memoir* by Vera Newman); Pelham Books Limited (*The Artless Musician* by Sidney Harrison); A D Peters (*Beachcomber*); Methuen and Co Ltd (*The Unashamed Accompanist* by Gerald Moore); The Editor, *The Evening News*, London; *Time* Magazine and Time-Life Incorporated; *Punch*; Mander and Mitchenson Theatre Collection; Mr Osbert Lancaster and Glyndebourne Festival Opera; and to the late Mr Gerard Hoffnung, and Dennis Dobson publishers of *The Hoffnung Music Festival*.

I feel sure that several of the Beecham stories that are part of the currency of musical small-talk were first put into circulation by Mr Neville Cardus.

If I have inadvertently omitted anyone to whom acknowledgement is due, I apologise here and now.

LESLIE AYRE